YOUR KNOWLEDGE HAS

- We will publish your bachelor's and
  master's thesis, essays and papers

- Your own eBook and book -
  sold worldwide in all relevant shops

- Earn money with each sale

Upload your text at www.GRIN.com
and publish for free

Sebastian Feil

Aus der Reihe: e-fellows.net stipendiaten-wissen

e-fellows.net (Hrsg.)

Band 1437

Dependencies among Software Development Teams. Coordination, Communication and Collaboration

GRIN Publishing

Imprint:

Copyright © 2014 GRIN Verlag GmbH
Print and binding: Books on Demand GmbH, Norderstedt Germany
ISBN: 978-3-656-97719-3

This book at GRIN:

http://www.grin.com/en/e-book/299929/dependencies-among-software-develop-ment-teams-coordination-communication

GRIN - Your knowledge has value

Since its foundation in 1998, GRIN has specialized in publishing academic texts by students, college teachers and other academics as e-book and printed book. The website www.grin.com is an ideal platform for presenting term papers, final papers, scientific essays, dissertations and specialist books.

Visit us on the internet:

http://www.grin.com/

http://www.facebook.com/grincom

http://www.twitter.com/grin_com

DEPENDENCIES AMONG SOFTWARE DEVELOPMENT TEAMS

Master Seminar Paper

Date of submission: May 5, 2014

                    by: Sebastian Feil

Table of contents

List of figures

List of abbreviations

e. g.   exempli gratia

1 Introduction

1.1 Motivation

In the past the way of working in business was different than nowadays. Tasks were mostly defined and given to the employees by the corresponding manager. After the tasks were distributed to the employees, they started working on them individually and nearly separately. This way of working was justified in the characteristics of the tasks since they were mostly not dependent of each other. However, these days the complexity of tasks increased significantly in comparison to former tasks, which as a consequence became more and more dependent of each other.

Exactly this development of dependencies between tasks can be applied to software and employees working together on software development: Software used to be developed rather individually or in small teams. In course of time the development of software became more and more complex and thus software dependencies became an important factor in software development and most software development is now performed by teams of software engineers working collaboratively to achieve the determined goals. As a consequence the teams, developing software, became more dependent of each other. (Arora & Goel, 2012, page 1)

Furthermore, maintenance and development costs are also higher because of the mentioned inevitable changes in software and hence software complexity. This also means that designing software also depends on how well the software is structured, so that collaboration, coordination and communication among the software development teams are an important aspect in developing software.(Breivold et al., 2008) These three aspects are also a consequence of the development from single software development to large-scale multi-team development.

So, teaching employees how to write programs concerning software development is not the only ability to learn anymore. What is more, developers need to conceive that it is very important to be able to write programs comprehensivly for others and to understand programs, written by others. However, a lot more important factor is that

1

developers must be able to work effeciently with others. This is due to the increased dependencies of software.(Arora & Goel, 2012, page 1)

1.2 Goal of the paper

The goal of this seminar paper is to find out which dependencies exist in software development teams. These dependencies and their consequences will be identified and defined. These findings will be gathered by a systematic literature review based on the guidelines of Kitchenham, which will be explained in the second chapter. After that these findings will serve as a reference for constructing a framework respectively model, which illustrates and summarizes the impact of the dependencies for the software development teams. What is more, the literature review and the built model will be finally the answer to the following two research questions of this paper:

Q1: What types of dependencies between software development teams are reported in the Information Systems and Software Engineering literature?

Q2: What are the current theories on effects of team interdependencies?

1.3 Structure of the paper

The first chapter describes the motivation, problem and goal of the seminar paper and serves as an introduction to the topic of this seminar paper. Moreover, the two research questions are illustrated, which will be answered in the further course of this paper. In the second chapter the applied research methodology will be explained. The main focus of this paper will lie on the third chapter, in which first software dependencies will be determined and then derived to software development teams. The fourth chapter will illustrate the constructed framework respectively model based on the key findings of the third chapter. The fifth and last chapter will be a summary of the seminar paper and evaluate the findings critically. What is more, it will be defined how the work of this paper could be continued.

2 Research methodology

For this seminar paper a systematic literature review methodology has been chosen, which is based on the guidelines of Kitchenham. This methodolgy has been especially chosen because some literature already exists about software dependencies as well as dependencies among software development teams. Furthermore, it is the goal to leverage the existing literature about the mentioned topics in order to answer the research questions ideally.

The following search engines have been used in order to find the relevant literature for this seminar paper:

- IEEE Xplore: http://ieeexplore.ieee.org

- AIS Electronic Library: http://aisel.aisnet.org

- Springerlink: http://link.springer.com

- EBSCO: http://search.ebscohost.com

The keywords for the related topic were "Dependency", "Interdependency", "Coordination", "Collaboration" and "Roles" and the keywords for the searching area were "Teams", "Software Development Teams", "Software Development", "Systems Development", "Team Performance" and "Programming Teams". After having defined these keywords, they were used to search in the above mentioned search engines. But, this resulted in hundreds of retrieved papers. In order to reduce the high number of papers and limit them to the only relevant ones, first only those were considered which were addressing topics concerning dependencies. Second, all papers were filtered out which were not referring to dependencies and software as well as dependencies and teams. Third, the abstract of the papers became relevant and helped to filter out approximately 50 papers so that in sum a much smaller number of papers were relevant for this seminar paper. Finally, all the relevant gathered papers were classified by their relevance in "relevance 1", "relevance 2" and "relevance 3". This classification process helped a lot for using the best relevant literature in this seminar paper.

3 Software dependencies resulting in team dependencies

In order to determine and understand software dependencies and the resulting dependencies among software development teams, it is important to get a comprehensive about dependencies in general. For this purpose the following figure has been slightly adjusted from the original one of Andrzej Duda and Chérif Keramane:

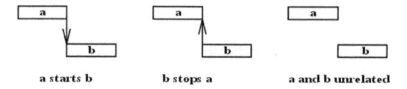

     a starts b   **b stops a**   **a and b unrelated**

Figure 1: What are dependencies based on (Duda & Keramane, 1995)

Figure 1 shows three different situations with each two variables "a" and "b". The first situation "a starts b" is a dependency because "b" is dependent of "a". This is true as "b" cannot start unless "a" has not finished. What is more, "b" stops "a" also illustrates a dependency between both variables. If "b" does not break "a", "a" will not stop doing its task and therefore "a" is dependent of "b". The last situation shows a state in which no dependency exits. Since "a" and "b" are unrelated to each other "a" and "b" are independent. This means that "a" and "b" can perform tasks independently.(Duda & Keramane, 1995)

To sum up, dependencies can be best explained by quoting Strode and Huff: "[a dependency is] a situation that occurs when the progress of one action relies upon the timely output of a previous action or the presence of a specific thing."(Strode, 2013)

3.1 Software dependencies

After having defined dependencies in general, this section will focus on the different dependencies of software, which are the basis for dependencies among software development teams. It is important to know that the literature suggests many dependencies regarded from different perspectives like source code, design or structure. Since analyzing all dependencies of software would be a research question for another paper, only selected dependencies of software will be presented in the following.

Before introducing the different dependency views, one view of software dependencies will be presented as a hypothesis first. This hypothesis has been chosen because the author of this paper believes that this view is the general comprehensive of software dependencies:

Ghezzi et al. believe that the more independent the modules of software are, the more independently software development teams can work (Ghezzi, Jazayeri, & Mandrioli, 2002, page 241). It is clearly noticeable, that they link software dependencies with modular components of software. In general, software modules are dependent of each other if a module relies on another module to conduct its operations (Spanoudakis & Zisman, 2004). What is more, Herbsleb et al. and Parnas have the same opinion and state that if one wants to lower software development teams' dependencies, the modular component dependencies need to be reduced (Herbsleb et al., 2000; Parnas, 1972). In the following, the key findings of two authors concerning software dependencies will be presented:

Futrell et al. differentiate between two dependencies in software development – internal and external dependencies (Futrell et al., 2002, page 340):

External dependencies include any connection to the results of other projects, which means that the software development has dependencies to higher-level or lower-level projects. This means that one's software development tasks may be dependent of e.g. hardware, installation or training. What is more, stakeholders can also be external dependencies. One example would be that one is dependent of them concerning financials. Another example for stakeholder dependency can be suppliers because one may be dependent of another software project which implements an interface to a third-party system for example which you need to use.(Futrell et al., 2002, page 340)

Internal dependencies are related to the software development project. These emerge in the form of dependencies between modules, components and processes since they are highly interrelated. They are a direct result of relationships between various components. Moreover, integral process dependencies are also internal ones like software quality audits etc.(Futrell et al., 2002, page 341)

5

Strode and Huff were focusing on internal dependencies in software development projects. They found out that there exists three major dependencies:

- "Knowledge dependency"

- "Task dependency"

- "Resource dependency" (Strode, 2013)

Knowledge dependency appears if any form of information is required to progress in a project. Strode and Huff identified four forms of knowledge dependency: "Requirement": This means that a requirement or domain knowledge is not known and must be identified. On top of that, this issue affects the software development process. The second form of knowledge dependency is "expertise": This appears during a situation where technical or task information is not known by everyone and this affects the software development process. Another form of knowledge dependency is "task allocation": Task allocation occurs when it is not known who is doing what and this affects the software development process. The last form of knowledge dependency is "historical": Historical is a situation in which knowledge about former decisions is required and this influences the software development process.(Strode, 2013)

Task dependency appears when one task needs to be finished before another task can be started, proceeded or finished during software development. Task dependency is differentiated between two forms: "Activity": This is a situation in which an activity cannot proceed because another activity has not been completed and this situation affects the software development process. The last form of task dependency is "business process": business process is a situation in which an existing business process causes activities to be proceeded in a certain order, which affects the software development process.(Strode, 2013)

The last of the three major identified dependencies by Strode and Huff is "resource dependency". Resource dependency is defined as the requirement of an object for the software development project to progress. Resource dependency is differentiated between two forms: "Entity": entity is a situation in which a resource like a person, place or thing is not availabe, which influences the software development process. The last form of resource dependency is "technical": this means that a technical aspect of the

6

software development affects the progress because one software component needs to interact with another software component and its availability affects the software development process.(Strode, 2013)

Based on the three major dependencies, which have been explained above, Diane Strode conducted an experiment, in which four different projects have been observed. Three of this project were an agile project and one was a non-agile project. Since the observations did not show a difference among all four projects, it can be assumed that the three dependencies can be applied to all software development projects. The goal of her research was to find out which of the three dependencies is dominant.(Strode, 2013)

The result of Strode's research indicates that the lack of information during software development affects the project more than any other form of dependencies. This means that the knowledge dependency, which is one of the three major dependencies, is the most important dependency to consider. What is more, she found out that averaged 73% of all dependencies in a project are related to knowledge dependencies. Out of these 73% approximately 58% of the dependencies are involving information acquisition like requirements, structure and function of existing systems or acquiring other people's expertise. Only 17% are task dependencies and only 10% of all dependencies are resource dependencies.(Strode, 2013)

These insights are partly suprising since the first thought of dependencies in software projects may rather be task or resource dependency. However, it is very important to consider that knowledge dependency sticks out.

As a consequence, knowledge dependency needs to be given highly attention. Furthermore, since knowledge dependency in software development projects is rather a team dependency than from technical nature, the further focus of this seminar paper must be set on software development teams. In order to handle this insight coordination, collaboration and communication become an important aspect for the further course of this paper.

In addition, in the beginning of this section one view of software dependencies have been presented, which was from technical nature (modular component software dependencies). This point of view has been broadened by Strode's research because she

7

found out that knowledge dependencies are even higher than technical dependencies. This insight means that at least on both dependencies must be focused during software development projects with multiple teams.

In order to consider technical and knowledge dependencies ideally, several researcher suggest solutions. For the dependencies resulting from technical nature (modular component dependency) Trainer et al. suggest to create a so called "call-graph with social information" (Trainer et al., 2005). This graph illustrates all developers and should help to create an overview which software developer of the software development team is dependent of another software developer who is responsible for a defined piece of code (de Souza et al., 2004). To get an understanding how this graph looks, it was attached to the appendix.

This graph helps to illustrate dependencies among the software development team concerning modular components. This is a big benefit because every software developer is aware of whom he or she is dependent of. On top of that, software developers are also able to see who depends on his or her work. In case of delays the software developer knows exactly who to contact. However, Trainer et al. claim correctly that there is still coordination, communication and collaboration effort required. (Trainer et al., 2005) Thus, these three aspects will be analyzed in the following sections.

3.2 Coordination among software development teams

The previous section revealed that knowledge and technical dependencies are an important factor to consider in software development projects. As described in the previous section Parnas was one of the researchers who found out that there are software developer dependencies because of modular dependencies within software development. What is more, he realized a relationship between software dependencies and coordination.(Parnas, 1972) The same applies to Strode's research. Her main insight was that knowledge dependencies are the dominating factor in software development projects. In order to handle knowledge dependencies she also mentions that there is a strong relationship between knowledge dependencies and coordination.(Strode, 2013) In the following coordination among software development teams will be investigated because as already described coordination is an important factor in software development with regard to dependencies.

First of all, it is necessary to define coordination in the dependency context. Nguyen-Duc and Cruzes define coordination "[…] as activities to manage dependencies between tasks and task holders [...]" (Nguyen-Duc & Cruzes, 2013). Malone and Crowston define coordination as "activities required to maintain consistency within the workflow" (Malone & Crowston, 1990). What is more, it can be inferred from these two coordination definitions that if there is no interdependency between activities, then there is nothing to coordinate (Malone & Crowston, 1994). Furthermore, in terms of coordination it is important to consider the organizational boundary because it cannot be assumed that all software development team members are from the same organization (Nguyen-Duc & Cruzes, 2013). Organizational boundary in this context means that there exists differences in functional and strategic concerns, role structure etc., which appear among organizational units (Espinosa et al., 2006). Curtis et al. observed that coordination across these organizational boundaries is extremely important in order to succeed the software development project. (Curtis et al., 1988)

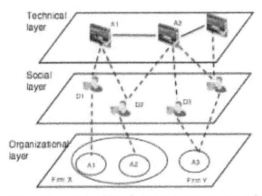

Figure 2: Organizational boundaries based on (Nguyen-Duc & Cruzes, 2013)

For the purpose to get a better comprehensive of organizational boundaries figure 2 has been attached to this paper. It visualizes the meaning of organizational boundaries. Task A1 and A2 from the technical layer are performed by developer D1 (task A1), developer D2 (task A1 as well as task A2) and developer D3 (task A2). The figure indicates that developer D1 and developer D2 belong to the same firm x, but are located in two different development units and developer D3 belongs to firm y. While it is clear that organizational distance can be expected between the two firms (x and y), it can also be assumed that there is also an organizational boundary between team A1 and A2. Since

9

these described aspects are not always considered in software development projects, many coordination problems occur. (Nguyen-Duc & Cruzes, 2013)

The following passage presents selected problems in order to understand how effective coordination needs to be performed:

- The identification of people who are technically interdepentend is hard, which complicates to define coordination requirements (Cataldo, et al., 2007; Damian & Zowghi, 2003)

- Due to high distances among sites, team coordination in a face-to-face manner is disabled (Anh et al., 2012)

- Communication and coordination of information takes too much time (Damian et al., 2007; Nidumolu, 1995)

In order to avoid these listed issues it will be illustrated how coordination can be best achieved in large-scale software development systems:

A framework for analysis of coordination is presented by the coordination theory, which defines coordination as the management of dependencies, which are to be managed by coordination mechanisms (Malone & Crowston, 1994; Scheerer et al., 2014). Espinosa et al. define three different types of coordination:

- Mechanistic

- Organic

- Cognitive coordination (Espinosa et al., 2010)

According to Espinosa et al. mechanistic coordination refers to coordination by plan or by program which use processes, routines or other practices like procedure manuals, interface specifications etc. to manage dependencies with little communication. This means that mechanistic coordination is most usable for task activities which are routine.(Espinosa et al., 2010)

Organic coordination refers to coordination by feedback or by mutual adjustment, which primarily uses coordination by communication and interaction. On top of that, this type of coordination is most valuable with non-routine and uncertain task activities. What is more, these task activities cannot be coordinated mechanistically as conditions often change. Organic coordination can be conducted in various forms like formal or informal, spontaneous or planned, verbal or non-verbal etc.(Espinosa et al., 2010)

Cognitive coordination is used when collaborators already have knowledge about each other as well as each other's tasks. The collaborators do not need to talk with each other because their knowledge about each other helps them to anticipate what the others probably do. This coordination type has many different forms, however all are based on shared knowledge which collaborators have about the task. Examples for cognitive coordination are transactive memory (who knows what) (Wegner, 1995), which is similar to expertise coordination, which means to know where expertise is located, where expertise is needed and how to create expertise (Faraj & Sproull, 2000).

Espinosa et al. view cognitive coordination as the most important factor for coordination mechanisms in multiteam systems (Espinosa et al., 2010). This point of view is also represented by some other authors. Scheerer et al. have build a conceptual framework, that indicates a process theoretical view of inter-team coordination effectiveness, in which the three described coordination mechanisms interplay (Scheerer et al., 2014). This framework, which has been attached to the appendix, depicts that mechanistic, organic and cognitive coordination only generate effectiveness when those interplay together. In this context, coordination effectiveness means "[…] to which extent dependencies among task activities are well managed" (Li & Maedche, 2012) .

Based on this framework Scheerer et al. built a coordination model, based on the three coordination mechanics, with several strategy types. Since only two strategy types and three subtypes are completely plausible, only those will be presented in the following: (Scheerer et al., 2014)

Strategy type 1 consists of high mechanistic, low organic and low cognitive coordination. This strategy type is seen theoretically as the perfect plan-based approach to software development. The focus of this coordination strategy type is highly on mechanistic coordination with a little communication between individuals. This means that at least one person must have a deep overview of the technical details of the entire software system. Indeed, this strategy type makes sense from a theoretical point of

11

view, but in practice it is rather utopistic because one person must have the capability to plan an entire software release down to individual work packages despite complex interdependencies in existing codebases.(Scheerer et al., 2014)

Strategy type 2 is the opposite of strategy type 1. Since mechanistic coordination only occurs low to medium, the focus of this strategy is on organic and cognitive mechanisms in order to achieve coordination effectiveness: (Scheerer et al., 2014)

Subtype 2.1 also called "organic planning" is focused on high organic as well as high cognitive coordination with medium mechanistic coordination. Characteristically for this subtype is that individuals have planning capability limits but still some planning is required in order to reduce communication and rework overhead as a consequence of organic coordination.(Scheerer et al., 2014)

Subtype 2.2 also called "communication focused" indicates very low mechanistic coordination but a high amount of organic and cognitive coordination. The very low mechanistic coordination is justified in the assumption that planning and setting rules is waste because they must be adjusted constantly. So that teams still achieve coordination effectiveness, they have to communicate understandably. Furthermore, they need to adjust their actions mutually, which is highly based on a common comprehensive and feedback.(Scheerer et al., 2014)

Subtype 2.3 also called "selective communication" shows low-medium mechanistic coordination, high organic coordination and medium cognitive coordination. It is important to know for this subtype that the organic coordination is limited to the number of individuals or teams that can be effectively coordinated. In this subtype strategy only subparts of the development system take part in coordination activities. Moreover, hierarchical procedures, in which the number of involved individuals is reduced the more teams or subparts are involved, establish system wide coordination. This lowers the necessary shared understanding among the participants and increases the organic coordination effectiveness. As a consequence, this subtype strategy allows sense and respond for a leadership paradigm as there is a lower reliance on upfront planning and rigid rules.(Scheerer et al., 2014)

As already mentioned above only two out of 8 strategy types have been presented. This is justified in the aspect that only the two revealed strategy types are practically usable (Scheerer et al., 2014). However, one of these not plausibly perfect fitting strategies needs to be mentioned: There is a strategy type called "extensive coordination" which means that mechanistic coordination, organic coordination and cognitive coordination are high. It is true that this would be the perfect situation as the software development project would be well coordinated. But, this strategy would mean high overhead costs for coordination with uncertain benefits compared to the other strategies.(Scheerer et al., 2014)

All in all, in this section the term coordination has been introduced especially in the context of managing dependencies. Furthermore, three different coordination mechanisms have been revealed in order to achieve coordination effectiveness. Based on these mechanisms several strategy types have been illustrated. Based on the dependencies, which need to be managed within the software development team, a coordination strategy needs to be chosen. How this could be conducted, will be illustrated in the fourth chapter. Since coordination is not the only aspect in managing dependencies, the next section will investigate to which extent collaboration and communication can influence these dependencies.

3.3 Communication and collaboration among software development teams

In section 3.2 it was explained how coordination and software dependencies interact. This fact was based on the findings of two researcher "Strode" and "Parnas" (Parnas, 1972; Strode, 2013). However, Conway notes that the structure of a software system strongly correlates with the communication needs of software developers (Conway, 1968). Furthermore, Morelli et al. and Sosa et al. also found out that there is a high correlation between the dependencies in software development and the communication needs among the software developers (Morelli et al., 1995; Sosa et al., 2002). This insight infers that software developers, which deal with high software dependencies, are probably more concerned in communication than individuals working on software projects with low dependencies. Given this fact dependencies determine the frequency of communication among software development team members.(Fonseca et al., 2006)

In literature, there is a common understanding among the authors concerning communication depending on software dependencies that communication affects the success of the software development project (Allen et al. 1980; Bin, 2009; Griffin & Hauser, 1992) What is more, Dougherty infers that a high frequency of communication occurs more often in successful software development projects than failed ones (Dougherty, 1987).

Thus, two communication approaches concerning software dependencies will be analyzed in the following. The first one from Morelli et al. investigates types of communication concerning software dependencies, whereas the second one from Sosa et al. analyzes the frequency of communication:

Morelli et al. define three types of communication:

- Coordination type

- Knowledge type

- Inspiration type (Morelli et al., 1995)

Coordination type communication means that team members transfer technical information in order to perform their work as well as coordinate their tasks. The goal of knowledge type communication is that team members learn and develop new skills through others as well as consult with one another. Lastly, inspiration type communication is from more managerial than technical nature. It is a communication type through which individuals should be motivated and inspired. (Morelli et al., 1995)

Morelli et al. conducted a research on these three communication types: They found out that knowledge-type and inspiration-type communication each occurred approximately 40% and coordination-type communication only occurred approximately 20% during a software project (Morelli et al., 1995). This result is not surprising because in section 3.1 it has already been found out that knowledge dependencies in software development are dominating. In order to manage this dependency it is clearly evident that knowledge-type and inspiration-type communication are essential.

Another research of how software development teams communicate is based on Sosa et al. They studied how dependencies are managed through communication, which is

14

influenced by factors like geographic dispersion, organizational bonds and the degree of team interdependence. Furthermore, they built a model in which they formulated several hypotheses about how communication frequency and media choice is influenced by geographic dispersion, organizational bonds and the degree of interdependence. What is more, they found out that communication is significantly dependent of the existence of strong organizational bonds, highly interdependent team members and the use of electronic communication media.(Sosa et al., 2002)

First of all, Sosa et al. agree to Loch and Terwiesch's opinion that the average communication frequency increases with the increasing level of uncertainty and dependency (Loch & Terwiesch, 1998; Sosa et al., 2002). Therefore, Sosa et al. investigated the communication frequency and communication media usage based on two major categories – "communication drivers" and "communication barriers".(Sosa et al., 2002)

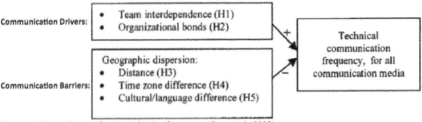

Figure 3: Determinants of communication frequency (Sosa et al., 2002)

As figure 3 illustrates Sosa et al. formulated five hypotheses, which state how the different factors of communication drivers and communication barriers affect the frequency of communication. In the following each hypothesis will be explained:

Communication drivers consist of team interdependencies and organizational bonds. According to Sosa et al., the higher the degree of team interdependence, the higher the communication frequency (H1) (Sosa et al., 2002). This is also reflected by other authors in literature who revealed that a greater degree of team interdependence leads to a greater communication effort (Adler, 1995).

In the beginning of chapter 3 organizational boundaries have been introduced. Within these boundaries individuals are subjected to organizational bonds. The second hypothesis of Sosa et al. is based on Allen et al., who found out that the technical communication of team members is increased by organizational bonds (Allen et al., 1980). Thus Sosa et al. formulated the second hypothesis (H2) in the following way: "Communication frequency is higher between individuals who share an organizational bond [...]" (Sosa et al., 2002).

Communication Barriers consist of three major types: Physical distance, time zone difference and cultural/language difference. Physical distance is understood as "[...] the relative distance between the facilities where the interacting team members are located"(Sosa et al., 2002). Sosa et al. state that "[...] communication frequency decreases with distance, independently of the communication media used" (H3) (Sosa et al., 2002). They justify this hypothesis by claiming that distance reduces face-to-face meetings and this strongly correlates with a decreased use of other media. (Sosa et al., 2002)

As fourth hypothesis Sosa et al. suggest that "communication frequency increases with overlapping working-time, independently of the communication media used" (H4) (Sosa et al., 2002). Since this hypothesis has been evaluated as an unimportant factor for the frequency of communication in the further research of Sosa et al., this hypothesis will not be considered in the further course of this paper. Finally, the last hypothesis was formulated as "communication frequency decreases with cultural/language differences, independently of the communication media used" (H5) (Sosa et al., 2002). An explanation for this hypothesis is that distance can be viewed as a proxy for culture, language and identity.(Sosa et al., 2002)

Based on these hypotheses Sosa et al. conducted a study in order to evaluate them. They found out that hypotheses H1 to H3 and H5 are valid. As already described in the previous passage H4 has been evaluated as a non-significant factor for the communication.(Sosa et al., 2002)

This chapter indicated various software dependencies, which resulted in software development team dependencies. Furthermore, in order to manage these dependencies coordination and communication are essential. In the next chapter, a model respectively framework will be built based on the key findings of this chapter. On the one hand this built model should serve as an overview of the key findings and on the other hand it should combine all factors in one model.

4 Software development teams dependencies model

In this chapter a dependencies model respectively framework will be presented, based on the key findings of the previous chapter. This model is derived from software dependencies, coordination, communication and collaboration insights. What is more, it should serve on the one hand as an overview and on the other hand generate new insights. Furthermore, through illustrating all findings from the previous chapter, the interplay of all these aspects is indicated.

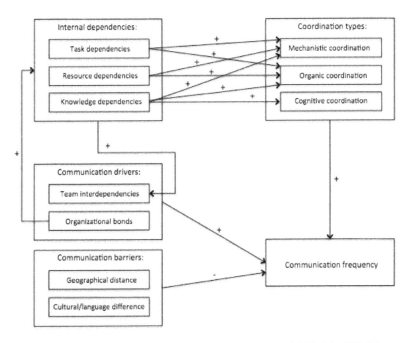

Figure 4: **Software development teams dependencies model based on** (Li & Maedche, 2012; Scheerer et al., 2014; Sosa et al., 2002; Strode, 2013)

Figure 4 shows this model/framework and links the key insights of the previous chapter with each other. Above these links, there is a plus, which means that the one aspect strengthens the corresponding one. However, this plus can be differently strong because it depends on the corresponding element. This means, that all the pluses are differently strong and it cannot be assumed that all factors influence the others equally. Same applies to the one minus. It depends on the geographical distance and cultural/language difference how strong it weakens the communication frequency.

17

In the following, first all important areas will be described again and second the interplay among them will be depicted. On the top of the left hand side of figure 4 it is presented the three dependencies, which can occur during software development. These three dependencies can be assigned to internal dependency. Indeed, there are also external dependencies, however they have been excluded because they do not have an effect on the software development team itself. Below the internal dependencies on the left side there are the communication drivers as well as communication barriers. They have been explained in chapter 3.3 and determine the communication frequency, which is situated on the right hand side below the factors of coordination. As described in chapter 3.2 coordination consists of mechanisitc coordination, organistic coordination and cognitive coordination. Based on the degree of the corresponding coordination type, a coordination strategy can be determined. Two of these coordination strategies as well as three subtypes of those have been explained in chapter 3.2. Furthermore, they can be found in the appendix. After all important areas of this model have been repeated in this passage, the interplay of those will be presented in the following.

As already mentioned internal dependencies, which occur during software development, are task dependencies, resource dependencies and knowledge dependencies. As described in section 3.1 task dependencies appear when one task needs to be finished before another task can be started, proceeded or finished. Resource dependencies represent the requirement of an object for software development projects to progress e.g. a resource is not available. Knowledge dependencies appear if any form of information is required to progress. (Strode, 2013) As illustrated in figure 4 the different dependency types affect the different coordination types: Both task dependency and resource dependency affect mechanistic coordination and organic coordination. This is justified because in a scenario in which a task depends on another task there must be some plans or processes which specify the coordination (mechanistic coordination). What is more, organic coordination is also needed because feedback and mutual adjustment are important, when one task is dependent of another one. Thus, the higher task dependency, the higher mechanistic and organic coordination. The same applies to resource dependency: If a resource like an employee is not available, this situation must be handled by processes and plans (mechanistic coordination) as well as feedback and mutual adjustment (organic coordination). That's why the higher resource dependency, the higher mechanistic and organic coordination. However, in contrast to task and

18

resource dependency knowledge dependency also affects cognitive coordination. This is justified in the fact that knowledge dependency includes that it is not known who does what and who knows what. In this case cognitive coordination is very important because it helps to coordinate where expertise is, how to create expertise and where expertise is needed. What is more, organic coordination is also necessary because if a requirement or domain knowledge is not known and must be identified it will be necessary to interact with others. On top of that, mechanistic coordination is also important as processes or procedure manuals for example can help if historical knowledge is needed. Therefore, depending on the type of knowledge dependency the higher knowledge dependency the higher mechanistic, organic and cognitive coordination. In addition, internal dependencies do not only affect coordination types, but also one factor of communication drivers. Team interdependencies are strengthened if task dependencies, resource dependencies or knowledge dependencies occur. Knowledge dependencies increase team interdependencies because if one does not know any fact, known from another one, he or she is dependent of the other one. Task dependencies also increase team interdependencies as if one is dependent of another one's task, team interdependencies will increase. On top of that, resource dependencies can also increase team interdependencies because if a resource is not available, another resource from the team is needed.

The second factor of communication drivers is organizational bonds. While internal dependencies affect team interdependencies, organizational boundaries affect internal dependencies. This is reasonable because the higher organizational boundaries the higher dependencies. For example the more parties are involved in a project, the more task dependencies exist. Thus, the higher organizational bonds, the higher internal dependencies. It is already known from the previous chapter that communication drivers consist of team interdependencies and organizational bonds, which affect communication frequency as well as that communication barriers consist of geographical distance and cultural/language difference. Since the affects of communication drivers and communication barriers on communication frequency have already been explained in the previous chapter, it will be skipped.

However, one affect on communication frequency is still missing. The three coordination types also influence communication frequency. Since the higher coordination is needed, the more communication will occur. However, the strength of the influence is determined on the height of mechanistic, organic and cognitive coordination. For example, communication frequency would be higher if organic coordination is the highest of the three than mechanistic coordination is the highest.

In this chapter, the author of this seminar paper illustrated a model, which was built on the basis of the previous chapter. This model combines all important aspects with regard to software development dependencies. This is a huge benefit because all aspects and models from the literature are not regarded separately. As illustrated in figure 4 many factors from different models interplay with others. Thus, the coordination effort, the communication frequency and impact of internal dependencies can be determined more precisely. However, since this model has not been proven yet, it must be regarded as a hypothesis, which is based on literature findings.

5 Conclusion

This seminar paper investigated the various dependencies among software development teams with the help of a systematic literature review.

In order to determine the influences of dependencies among software development teams, first software dependencies in the software development have been analyzed. Based on the insights of the software dependencies research, three major software dependencies have been found out: Knowledge dependency, task dependency and resource dependency. However, it must be considered that these three dependencies only represent a subset of many others, which have not been illustrated. What is more, during the research of software dependencies, it became evident that software dependencies could be an own research topic. In addition, only internal dependencies have been considered in the further course of this paper after section 3.1 as they have most influence on software development teams. Although external dependencies are not much relevant for software development teams, it needs to be kept in mind that those have been excluded.

After the dependencies of software have been determined, three coordination types have been demonstrated: Mechanistic coordination, organic coordination and cognitive coordination. The degree of these coordination types determines the corresponding coordination strategy type. Based on Scheerer et al. two strategy types and three subtypes of one strategy type have been presented.

After that, the factors, which determine the communication frequency, have been introduced. The main finding of this section was that team interdependency and organistational bonds are key drivers for the communication frequency, whereas geographical dispersion weakens the communication frequency.

Finally, all insights from the seminar paper have been represented in one model respectively framework, built by the author of this paper. It indicated that the internal dependencies, the coordination types and communication drivers as well as communication barriers strongly interplay. Moreover, this model has been created based on the results of the literature review, which means that it cannot be assumed automatically that this model is valid in practice. Since it has never been proven in a case study, it needs to be regarded as a hypothesis. Additionally, in this model only internal dependencies of software development projects have been included. It can be assumed that external dependencies of software development projects could be integrated. This is a valid remark because external dependencies could also have an influence on communication freuquency and maybe coordination. This aspect needs to be analyzed in future work. What is more, the other internal dependencies, which have not been considered in this paper, could also have an influence on coordination and communication frequency so that this would also need to be regarded in a future paper.

What is more, it must be also regarded that this seminar paper is based on a literature review. This means that the constructed model has been built by many different sources and many opinions have been combined. Thus, this model can be viewed from a theoretical perspective as valid because many others have been the same opinion. However, as already mentioned the created model needs to be questioned in practice.

In addition, only the aspect "communication frequency" has been analyzed. But this aspect could be investigated more granularily. For example, it could be the case that frequency decreased in total, but the distribution of communication media changed like face-to-face meetings decreased by 90%, whereas e-mail communication increased by 80%. The results of this investigation would also be good to know since it could be the

21

case that the different degrees of coordination types change the distribution of communication frequency and through this new dependencies among software development teams could be created.

As a result, this seminar paper should serve as a first overview of the determinants of dependencies among software development teams and the resulting consequences. However, it must be kept in mind that future investigations are essential and need to be done. Furtheremore, it is important to prove the built model by a case study.

Bibliography

Adler, P. S. (1995). Interdepartmental Interdependence and Coordination: The Case of the Design/Manufacturing Interface. *Organization Science, 6*(2), 147–167. doi:10.1287/orsc.6.2.147

Allen, T. J., Lee, D. M. S., & Tushman, M. L. (1980). R #x0026;D performance as a function of internal communication, project management, and the nature of the work. *Engineering Management, IEEE Transactions on, EM-27*(1), 2–12. doi:10.1109/TEM.1980.6447372

Anh, N. D., Cruzes, D. S., & Conradi, R. (2012). Dispersion, coordination and performance in global software teams: A systematic review. In *Empirical Software Engineering and Measurement (ESEM), 2012 ACM-IEEE International Symposium on* (pp. 129–138). doi:10.1145/2372251.2372274

Arora, R., & Goel, S. (2012). Learning to Write Programs with Others: Collaborative Quadruple Programming. In *Software Engineering Education and Training (CSEE T), 2012 IEEE 25th Conference on* (pp. 32–41). doi:10.1109/CSEET.2012.27

Bin, G. (2009). Moderating Effects of Task Characteristics on Information Source Use: An Individual-level Analysis of R&D Professionals in New Product Development. *J. Inf. Sci., 35*(5), 527–547. doi:10.1177/0165551509105196

Breivold, H. P., Crnkovic, I., Land, R., & Larsson, S. (2008). Using dependency model to support software architecture evolution. In *Automated Software Engineering - Workshops, 2008. ASE Workshops 2008. 23rd IEEE/ACM International Conference on* (pp. 82–91). doi:10.1109/ASEW.2008.4686324

Cataldo, M., Bass, M., Herbsleb, J. D., & Bass, L. (2007). On Coordination Mechanisms in Global Software Development. In *Global Software Engineering, 2007. ICGSE 2007. Second IEEE International Conference on* (pp. 71–80). doi:10.1109/ICGSE.2007.33

Conway, M. E. (1968). How Do Committees Invent? *Datamation.* Retrieved from http://www.melconway.com/research/committees.html

Curtis, B., Krasner, H., & Iscoe, N. (1988). A Field Study of the Software Design Process for Large Systems. *Commun. ACM, 31*(11), 1268–1287. doi:10.1145/50087.50089

Damian, D. E., & Zowghi, D. (2003). RE challenges in multi-site software development organisations. *Requir. Eng., 8*(3), 149–160. Retrieved from http://dblp.uni-trier.de/db/journals/re/re8.html#DamianZ03

Damian, D., Marczak, S., & Kwan, I. (2007). Collaboration Patterns and the Impact of Distance on Awareness in Requirements-Centred Social Networks. In *Requirements Engineering Conference, 2007. RE '07. 15th IEEE International* (pp. 59–68). doi:10.1109/RE.2007.51

De Souza, C. R. B., Redmiles, D., Cheng, L.-T., Millen, D., & Patterson, J. (2004). How a Good Software Practice Thwarts Collaboration: The Multiple Roles of APIs in Software Development. *SIGSOFT Softw. Eng. Notes, 29*(6), 221–230. doi:10.1145/1041685.1029925

Dougherty, D. J. (1987). *New Products in Old Organizations: The Myth of the Better Mousetrap in Search of the Beaten Path.* Massachusetts Institute of Technology. Retrieved from http://books.google.de/books?id=_vjbtgAACAAJ

Duda, A., & Keramane, C. (1995). Structured Temporal Composition of Multimedia Data. In *In Proc. IEEE International Workshop on Multimedia- Database- Management Systems, Blue Mountain Lake.*

Espinosa, J. A., Armour, F., & Boh, W. F. (2010). Coordination in Enterprise Architecting: An Interview Study. In *System Sciences (HICSS), 2010 43rd Hawaii International Conference on* (pp. 1–10). doi:10.1109/HICSS.2010.450

Espinosa, J. A., DeLone, W. H., & Lee, G. (2006). Global boundaries, task processes and IS project success: a field study. *IT & People, 19*(4), 3@article{Curtis:1988:FSS:50087.50089, author = {C. Retrieved from http://dblp.uni-trier.de/db/journals/itp/itp19.html#EspinosaDL06

Faraj, S., & Sproull, L. (2000). Coordinating Expertise in Software Development Teams. *Management Science, 46*(12), pp. 1554–1568. Retrieved from http://www.jstor.org/stable/2661533

Fonseca, S. B., de Souza, C. R. B., & Redmiles, D. F. (2006). Exploring the Relationship between Dependencies and Coordination to Support Global Software Development Projects. In *Global Software Engineering, 2006. ICGSE '06. International Conference on* (p. 243). doi:10.1109/ICGSE.2006.261241

Futrell, R. T., Shafer, D. F., Shafer, L., & Online, S. T. B. (2002). *Quality software project management.* Upper Saddle River, NJ: Prentice Hall.

Ghezzi, C., Jazayeri, M., & Mandrioli, D. (2002). *Fundamentals of Software Engineering* (2nd ed.). Upper Saddle River, NJ, USA: Prentice Hall PTR.

Griffin, A., & Hauser, J. R. (1992). Patterns of Communication Among Marketing, Engineering and Manufacturing—A Comparison Between Two New Product Teams. *Management Science, 38*(3), 360–373. doi:10.1287/mnsc.38.3.360

Herbsleb, J. D., Mockus, A., Finholt, T. A., & Grinter, R. E. (2000). Distance, Dependencies, and Delay in a Global Collaboration. In *Proceedings of the 2000 ACM Conference on Computer Supported Cooperative Work* (pp. 319–328). New York, NY, USA: ACM. doi:10.1145/358916.359003

Li, Y., & Maedche, A. (2012). Formulating Effective Coordination Strategies in Agile Global Software Development Teams. In *ICIS.* Association for Information Systems. Retrieved from http://dblp.uni-trier.de/db/conf/icis/icis2012.html#LiM12

Loch, C. H., & Terwiesch. (1998). Communication and uncertainty in concurrent engineering. *Management Science, 44*(8), 1032–1048.

Malone, T. W., & Crowston, K. (1990). What is Coordination Theory and How Can It Help Design Cooperative Work Systems? In *Proceedings of the 1990 ACM Conference on Computer-supported Cooperative Work* (pp. 357–370). New York, NY, USA: ACM. doi:10.1145/99332.99367

Malone, T. W., & Crowston, K. (1994). The Interdisciplinary Study of Coordination. *ACM Comput. Surv., 26*(1), 87–119. doi:10.1145/174666.174668

Morelli, M. D., Eppinger, S. D., & Gulati, R. K. (1995). Predicting technical communication in product development organizations. *Engineering Management, IEEE Transactions on, 42*(3), 215–222. doi:10.1109/17.403739

Nguyen-Duc, A., & Cruzes, D. S. (2013). Coordination of Software Development Teams across Organizational Boundary -- An Exploratory Study. In *Global Software Engineering (ICGSE), 2013 IEEE 8th International Conference on* (pp. 216–225). doi:10.1109/ICGSE.2013.35

Nidumolu, S. (1995). The Effect of Coordination and Uncertainty on Software Project Performance: Residual Performance Risk as an Intervening Variable. *Information Systems Research, 6*(3), 191–219. doi:10.1287/isre.6.3.191

Parnas, D. L. (1972). On the Criteria to Be Used in Decomposing Systems into Modules. *Commun. ACM, 15*(12), 1053–1058. doi:10.1145/361598.361623

Scheerer, A., Hildenbrand, T., & Kude, T. (2014). Coordination in Large-Scale Agile Software Development: A Multiteam Systems Perspective. In *System Sciences (HICSS), 2014 47th Hawaii International Conference on* (pp. 4780–4788). doi:10.1109/HICSS.2014.587

Sosa, M. E., Eppinger, S. D., Pich, M., McKendrick, D. G., & Stout, S. K. (2002). Factors that influence technical communication in distributed product development: an empirical study in the telecommunications industry. *Engineering Management, IEEE Transactions on, 49*(1), 45–58. doi:10.1109/17.985747

Spanoudakis, G., & Zisman, A. (2004). Software Traceability: A Roadmap. In *Handbook of Software Engineering and Knowledge Engineering* (pp. 395–428). World Scientific Publishing.

Strode, D. (2013). Extending the Dependency Taxonomy of Agile Software Development. In P. Antunes, M. Gerosa, A. Sylvester, J. Vassileva, & G.-J. Vreede (Eds.), *Collaboration and Technology* (Vol. 8224, pp. 274–289). Springer Berlin Heidelberg. doi:10.1007/978-3-642-41347-6_20

Trainer, E., Quirk, S., de Souza, C., & Redmiles, D. (2005). Bridging the Gap Between Technical and Social Dependencies with Ariadne. In *Proceedings of the 2005 OOPSLA Workshop on Eclipse Technology eXchange* (pp. 26–30). New York, NY, USA: ACM. doi:10.1145/1117696.1117702

Wegner, D. M. (1995). A computer network model of human transactive memory, *13*, 1–21.

Appendix

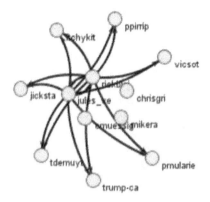

Figure 5: Call-graph with social information (Trainer et al., 2005)

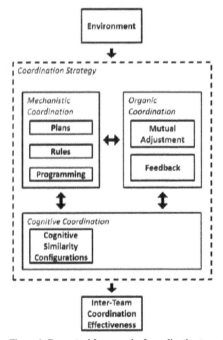

Figure 6: Conceptual framework of coordination types (Scheerer et al., 2014)

Strategy Type	Coordination type			plausible
	Mechanistic	Organic	Cognitive	
1	high	low	low	✓
2	low	high	high	✓
3	low	low	high	(✓)
4	high	high	high	(✓)
5	low	low	low	(✓)
6	low	high	low	-
7	high	high	low	-
8	high	low	high	-

Figure 7: Strategy types of coordination (Scheerer et al., 2014)

Strategy Type	Coordination type			plausible
	Mechanistic	Organic	Cognitive	
2.1	medium	high	high	✓
2.2	very low	high	high	✓
2.3	low-medium	high	medium	✓

Figure 8: Sub-strategy types (Scheerer et al., 2014)

www.ingramcontent.com/pod-product-compliance
Lightning Source LLC
LaVergne TN
LVHW042306060326
832902LV00009B/1301